THE GREEN–FINGERED GARDENER
containers

a practical guide to creating beautiful
pots for every season

stephanie donaldson

southwater

This edition is published by Southwater

Southwater is an imprint of Anness Publishing Ltd
Hermes House, 88–89 Blackfriars Road,
London SE1 8HA
tel. 020 7401 2077; fax 020 7633 9499
www.southwaterbooks.com; info@anness.com

© Anness Publishing Ltd 2001, 2003

This edition distributed in the UK by The Manning Partnership Ltd,
6 The Old Dairy, Melcombe Road, Bath BA2 3LR;
tel. 01225 478 444; fax 01225 478 440; sales@manning-partnership.co.uk

This edition distributed in the USA and Canada by National Book Network,
4501 Forbes Boulevard, Suite 200, Lanham, MD 20706;
tel. 301 459 3366; fax 301 429 5746; www.nbnbooks.com

This edition distributed in Australia by Pan Macmillan Australia,
Level 18, St Martins Tower, 31 Market St, Sydney, NSW 2000;
tel. 1300 135 113; fax 1300 135 103; customer.service@macmillan.com.au

A CIP catalogue record for this book is available from the British Library.

Publisher: Joanna Lorenz
Managing Editor: Judith Simons
Project Editor: Emma Hardy
Designer: Ian Sandom
Photographers: Marie O'Hara,
Janine Hosegood, John Freeman
Stylist: Stephanie Donaldson

Previously published as *Container Gardening*

1 3 5 7 9 10 8 6 4 2

THE GREEN-FINGERED GARDENER
containers

introduction

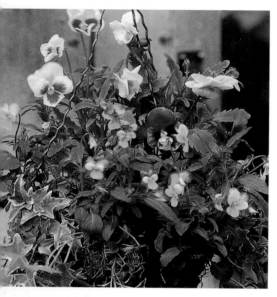

ABOVE: *Hanging baskets filled with pansies create a lovely focal point of gentle colour.*

BELOW: *Create impact in the garden by colour-theming seasonal plantings to tune in with their surroundings. This works best with plants in containers whose colours can be chosen to complement the flowers.*

Container gardening commends itself on many levels. For one thing, it is a highly convenient form of gardening. You do not need to be a full-time gardener with a large country garden to grow the lushest, tastiest herbs and summer berries, or beautiful flowers of every form and hue. Where flowerbed plants remain more or less fixed in their positions throughout the year, the beauty of containers is that with minimum effort they will instantly jazz up a balcony or roof garden, extend the garden into an area of shady paving outside the back door and liven up window sills with colour, scent and shape. They can also, of course, be used indoors, and can be easily moved around, allowing the plants currently at their best to take centre-stage.

Problems of limited space are easily overcome with the use of the vertical as well as the horizontal plane, which is almost uniquely possible with the use of containers, such as hanging baskets and window boxes. Another advantage is that gardening with containers allows you to transcend the limitations of your own local soil and to control the watering of your plants to a much higher degree.

Quite apart from the convenience, however, container gardening opens horizons of horticultural creativity that are closed to purely flowerbed-based gardening. You can, for example, bring elaborate and visually stunning gardening to a window box many stories up. Hanging baskets allow you to suspend great glowing orbs of colour and scent at head height, where they cannot fail to make an impression. While few of us would be able to afford the large and elegant open spaces we might perhaps feel our gardening talents deserve, the equivalent in terms of pots and planters is cheap and readily available.

Containers also offer scope for originality and eccentricity. They can be made from scratch, redecorated, or even fashioned from such things as a worn-out copper boiler. Shops and garden centres stock an ever-increasing range of containers to suit every budget, from magnificent Italian olive jars to humble plastic pots. Junk shops and car boot sales are also a rich source of objects that can take on a new lease of life as a planter.

In the following pages you will find scores of imaginative themes and ideas for beautiful containers. Don't be dismayed if you can't find exactly the plants suggested – there is nearly always an excellent alternative. With a little experience, you'll soon be able to create your own eye-catching arrangements.

ABOVE: *Sunflowers grow very well in pots provided you are not growing the giant varieties. Grow your own from seed; there are many kinds to choose from, including the one with double flowers used here.*

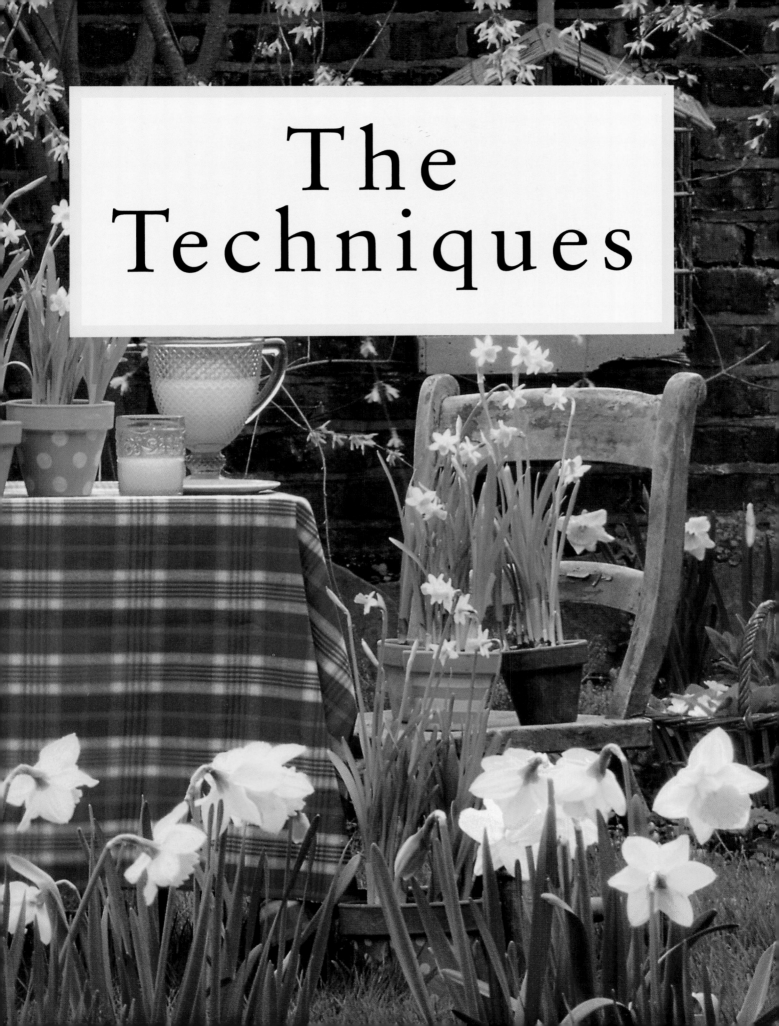

The Techniques

Types of Container

One of the challenges of container gardening is finding the right container for the right setting. You can now quite readily buy a whole range of lovely containers, for example, waist-high, Italian olive oil jars make a terrific focal point – big and bold and stylish. At the other end of the scale, you can be as imaginative as you like. You could use a Wellington boot or an old shoe for an engaging, quirky touch. In between, of course, the choice is huge: rustic terracotta, voguish metal or brightly painted tins, Mediterranean style.

It is important to consider the final setting when you are buying a container. A rustic tub may look charming under the window of a thatched cottage, but inappropriate outside a formal town house. Bear proportions in mind and, for example, choose a window box that exactly fits the sill. It is also worth noting that the weight of a container, when filled with compost and freshly watered, will be considerably greater than when empty. Think twice before packing your roof terrace or balcony with heavy pots: the structure may not be able to cope. And never leave a container on a window-sill from where it could fall down into the street.

Stone troughs

NOT SO READILY AVAILABLE BUT DEFINITELY WORTH LOOKING AT.

Advantages – durable and attractive.

Disadvantages – very heavy and expensive.

Pots and barrels

VERSATILE AND PRACTICAL.

Advantages – maintenance-free and versatile.

Disadvantages – heavy to move.

Wooden window boxes

GIVE A WOODEN CONTAINER AN ORIGINAL LOOK WITH YOUR OWN COLOUR SCHEME.

Advantages – you can change the look to suit any new planting scheme.

Disadvantages – the boxes require occasional maintenance.

Terracotta window boxes

AVAILABLE IN A WIDE RANGE OF SIZES AND STYLES.

Advantages – look good and appear even better with age.

Disadvantages – heavy, and may be damaged by frost.

Types of Hanging Basket

Galvanized tin

TIN HAS MOVED FROM THE UTILITARIAN TO THE FASHIONABLE.

Advantages – an interesting variation from the usual materials.

Disadvantages – drainage holes required.

Lightweight fibre window boxes

PLAIN AND PRACTICAL.

Advantages – look rustic, and have a rich brown colour.

Disadvantages – short life-span.

Baskets

CAN BE USED AS WINDOW BOXES PROVIDED THEY ARE GENEROUSLY LINED WITH MOSS BEFORE PLANTING.

Advantages – lightweight and attractive.

Disadvantages – plant pots must be removed for watering, or the base of the basket will be soaked and rot.

Before you choose the plants and how to arrange them, decide what style of hanging basket you are going to display them in. Garden centres stock a huge variety, which are all easy to work with and hang. Hanging baskets are made from plastic-coated wire, wrought iron and galvanized wire. Plants can also look great trailing from window boxes.

Hanging baskets

VARIED AND PRACTICAL.

Advantages – look lovely planted.

Disadvantages – need to be lined before use.

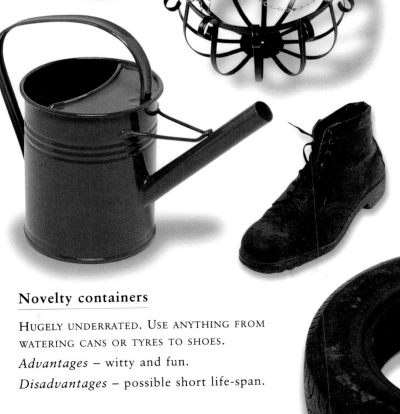

Novelty containers

HUGELY UNDERRATED. USE ANYTHING FROM WATERING CANS OR TYRES TO SHOES.

Advantages – witty and fun.

Disadvantages – possible short life-span.

11

Propagation Techniques

Most containers and plants are available from garden centres but raising your own plants from seed or cuttings is far easier than you may think and can be very rewarding. Buying young plants from mail order catalogues is an increasingly popular way of starting a collection.

Seed Sowing

One of the cheapest ways of getting a mass planting is by growing plants from seed. It is fun, can be easy (when growing marigolds, for instance), and you don't need a high-tech greenhouse. Furthermore, if you get hooked on the plants, you can collect your own ripe seed in the autumn for a spring sowing the following year.

Cuttings

If you want to increase your stock of the plants you are already growing in the garden, you can get quick results by taking spring cuttings.

When the cuttings have rooted – this will be immediately obvious because they suddenly perk up – wait for the roots to fill the pot, and then transfer to individual pots.

1 Fill the seed tray with seed compost. Gently firm and level the surface by pressing down on the compost using a tray of the same size. When sowing large seeds, such as sunflowers or marigolds, use a dibber, cane or pencil to make holes for each seed. Plant the seeds and cover with compost.

2 When sowing small seeds they should be thinly scattered on the surface of the compost and then covered with just enough sieved sand and compost to conceal them. Firm the surface, using another tray. Water from above, using a fine rose on a watering can, or by standing the tray in water until the surface of the compost is moist.

1 Remove the new soft-wood growth when it is about 10 cm (4 in) long, just above a leaf node.

2 Using a sharp knife, trim the cutting just below a node and trim away the lower leaves.

3 Dip the end of the stem in hormone rooting powder, and plant up in a small container, using cuttings compost.

4 Fill the pot with cuttings, water, and place in a warm, bright place, out of scorching sunlight.

3 Enclose the seed tray in a plastic jar or bag to conserve moisture and cover with a black plastic bag, as most seeds germinate best in a warm dark place.

4 Check daily and bring into the light when the seedlings are showing.

5 To create a moist microclimate for the cuttings, it's a good idea to enclose the pot completely in a plastic bag. Secure it with an elastic band around the pot.

Mail Order

Send off each year for the latest seed and plant catalogues. You will invariably find a wider range than you can buy in a garden centre. Young plants are packed into special packages, which minimize damage during transit, but as they are restricted and in the dark they are initially weakened and some care is necessary to encourage vigorous growth.

1 Open the package with care. Leaves will probably unfold from the confined space. Each plant should be intact and clearly labelled.

2 Lift the plants out of their travelling box. Labels tucked underneath the root ball reduce the necessity for handling it directly and helps to keep the compost intact.

3 Plant in a small pot. If the plants seem very wilted, remove some of the larger leaves.

Potting On

After several weeks your young plants, whether grown from seed, mail order stock or cuttings, will need potting on. This simply means giving the young plant its own larger, individual container.

1 Young plants are ready to move into larger pots when the roots start to emerge through the holes in the base of the pot. Gently remove the rootball from the pot to check. If there is more than one seedling in the pot, carefully tease away each individual rootball. (Some plants hate to have their roots disturbed. The information on the seed packet will tell you this. These seeds are best sown individually in peat pots or modular trays.) Lower the rootball of the plant into a pot marginally bigger than the existing one.

2 Holding the plant carefully so as not to damage the stem, gently pour potting compost around the rootball, firming lightly.

3 Dibble the compost down the side of the pot to eliminate air spaces. It does not matter if the stem of the seedling is buried deeper than it was previously, as long as the leaves are well clear of the soil. Water, using a can with a fine rose.

Composts

Composts come in various formulations suitable for different plant requirements. A standard potting compost is usually peat-based and is suitable for all purposes. Peat and peat substitutes are relatively light in weight, and are therefore the obvious choice for hanging baskets. Regular watering is vital when using peat-based composts, as it is very difficult to moisten them again if they have been allowed to dry out completely. Different composts can be mixed together for specific plant needs.

Standard compost

The majority of composts available at garden centres are peat-based with added fertilizers.

Ericaceous compost

A peat-based compost with no added lime, essential for rhododendrons, camellias and heathers in containers.

Container compost

A peat-based compost with moisture-retaining granules and added fertilizer, specially formulated for window boxes and containers.

Peat-free compost

Manufacturers now offer a range of composts using materials from renewable resources such as coir fibre. They are used in the same way as peat-based composts.

Loam-based compost

Uses sterilized loam as the main ingredient, with fertilizers to supplement the nutrients in the loam. Although much heavier than peat-based compost, it can be lightened by mixing with peat-free compost. Ideal for long-term planting as it retains nutrients well.

THE ESSENTIAL FERTILIZER ELEMENTS

All plant fertilizers contain three key elements, nitrogen (N), phosphorous (P), and potassium/potash (K), with extra trace elements. These three promote, respectively, foliage growth, flower development, and fruit ripening and root development.

When buying a packet of fertilizer you can easily check the balance of the ingredients. It is printed as an "NPK" ratio, for instance 12:5:12. But don't be fooled into thinking that a reading of 24:10:24 is stronger, giving twice the value. It won't, of course, as the ratio is the same. A fertilizer with a ratio of 10:5:10 provides a sound, balanced diet. (You can purchase meters from garden centres that give a guide to the nutrient levels in the soil but they are not, to date, particularly accurate.)

Besides feeding, you can also trick some plants into a prolific display of flowering. Plants packed into small containers, with restricted (but not crippling) root space, feel that they are in danger of dying. Their immediate response is to do what all flowering plants are programmed to do – flower and set seed to continue the species.

Feeding Container Plants

It is not generally understood that most potting composts contain sufficient food for only six weeks of plant growth. After that, the plants will slowly starve unless more food is introduced. There are several products available, all of which are easy to use. Many of the projects in this book use slow-release plant food granules because they are the easiest and most reliable way of ensuring your plants receive sufficient food during the growing season. For these granules to be effective the compost needs to remain damp or the nutrients cannot be released.

Slow-release Plant Food Granules

These will keep your container plants in prime condition and are very easy to use. One application lasts six months, whereas most other plant foods need to be applied fortnightly. Follow the manufacturer's recommended dose carefully; additional fertilizer will simply leach away.

BELOW: *A variety of plant foods (clockwise from top left): liquid foliar feed, two types of pelleted slow-release plant food granules, a general fertilizer and loose slow-release plant food granules.*

TOP: *Slow-release plant food granules can be added to the compost or potting mix in the recommended quantity before filling the container and planting it.*

ABOVE: *When adding fertilizer granules to the soil, sprinkle them on to the surface of the compost and rake into the top layer. Pelleted granules should be pushed approximately 2 cm (3/4 in) below the surface.*

Watering Container Plants

Watering plants in containers is an acquired art, and an incredibly important one. You cannot leave it entirely to nature because rain tends to bounce off the leaves of the bushiest plants, soaking not into the pot but into the adjoining ground.

Outside, pot plants dry out very quickly on roasting hot days. Unlike plants in the ground, their roots are encircled by heat; some thirsty plants might even need two waterings a day, so keep checking. You have to get the balance right between over- and under-watering.

Trial and error is one way, but there are a few key tips, one of the best and simplest being to stick your finger deep into the soil to test for dryness. If you are unsure, wait until you see the first signs of wilting, then give the plant a thorough drink, letting the water drain out of the bottom of the pot. And always water plants either first thing in the morning or, better still, late at night, so that the moisture does not quickly evaporate. At all costs, try to avoid over-watering, which is a bigger killer than pests and diseases combined.

The best water is either rainwater or cold, boiled water, but it is not essential to use these unless your tap water is very hard, or you are growing lime-hating plants such as camellias. Don't allow your potted plants to become waterlogged. If there is any water remaining in the saucer half an hour after watering, tip it away.

Window Boxes and Pots

Don't rush the watering. Though you might think one soaking is enough for a big window box, it might only wet the top few inches of compost. Wait until the water sluices out of the bottom. Container composts include a water-retaining gel and if the compost remains wet in cold weather it can cause the roots to rot.

Hanging Baskets

Summer hanging baskets need daily watering even in overcast weather and on a hot day should be watered morning and evening. Once they have been allowed to dry out it can be difficult for the compost to re-absorb water. In these circumstances it is a good idea to immerse hanging baskets in a large bucket or bowl of water. Winter and spring hanging baskets should be watered only when the soil is dry.

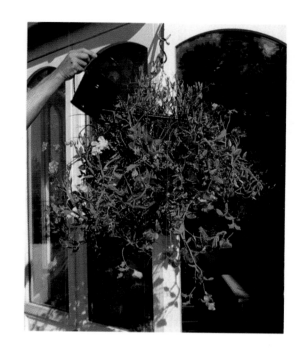

LEFT: *Houseplants enjoy being sprayed with water, but in hard water areas you should use rainwater or bottled water.*

Water-retaining Gel

One of the main problems for most container gardeners is the amount of watering required to keep the plants thriving in the growing season. Adding water-retaining gels to compost will certainly help reduce this task. Sachets of gel are available from garden centres.

1 Pour the recommended amount of water into a bowl.

2 Scatter the gel over the surface, stirring occasionally until it has absorbed the water.

3 Add to your compost at the recommended rate, and mix the gel in thoroughly before using it for planting.

MULCHES

A mulch is a layer of protective material placed over the soil. It helps to retain moisture, conserve warmth, suppress weeds and prevent soil splash on foliage and flowers.

Bark chippings

Bark is an extremely effective mulch and as it rots down it conditions the soil. It works best when spread at least 7.5 cm (3 in) thick and is therefore not ideal for small containers. It is derived from renewable resources.

Clay granules

Clay granules are widely used for hydroculture, but can also be used to mulch houseplants. When placing a plant in a *cachepot*, fill all around the pot with granules. When watered, the granules absorb moisture, which is then released slowly to create a moist microclimate for the plant.

Gravel

Gravel makes a decorative mulch for container plants, and also provides the correct environment for plants such as alpines. It is available in a variety of sizes and colours which can be matched to the scale and colours of the plants used.

Stones

Smooth stones can be used as decorative mulch for large container-grown plants. You can save stones dug out of the garden, collect your own from beaches and riverbeds or buy stones from garden centres. They also deter cats from using the soil as a litter tray.

Planting Pots

Planting up a container of any size could not be easier, as long as you follow a few basic rules. First, terracotta pots need a layer of material at the bottom to help the water drain away quickly. Plastic pots usually have sufficient drainage holes. Second, always plant into the appropriate size pot; that is, slightly larger than the rootball. Putting a small plant into a large pot is counter productive. The plant will put on good root growth at the expense of flowers and foliage. Since the hungry root system will drink up water rapidly in summer, check regularly that the soil is not too dry.

ABOVE: *Beautiful, elegant urns do not always need the finest flowering plants. As these twin pots show, even a modest planting works well. Indeed, it is often preferable because it does not detract from the gorgeous containers.*

Maintaining Plants

Large plants can grow in surprisingly small containers. They will not grow to the same height as if they were given a free root run, but should be impressive nonetheless. If possible, remove the top layer of soil every year, and replace it with fresh compost. There comes a time, however, when most plants finally outgrow their containers. What then? You can replace the mature plant with a cutting and start again. Alternatively, stick instead to plants that are slow-growing, or which will not rapidly fill their pots with roots. Or root prune.

Root pruning is a remarkably easy technique, which involves removing the plant from the pot in spring, when it is beginning to put on good growth. Either slice away the exterior of the rootball quite boldly, or snip at it with secateurs. Then replace in the existing pot, filling the gap with fresh compost.

Overwintering

Remember that while tender plants may just survive winter outside in your area, with their roots protected deep below ground, those in pots are much less likely to survive. The roots will be just the width of the pot (a few centimetres) away from encircling snow or icy winds. Bring these plants indoors or, if you do not have room, take cuttings before the end of the season.

Planting in Terracotta

Terracotta containers are always popular, but need some preparation before planting.

1 With terracotta it is essential to provide some form of drainage material in the base of the container. When planting in large pots or boxes, recycle broken-up polystyrene plant trays as drainage material. Lumps of polystyrene are excellent for this purpose and as they retain warmth they are of additional benefit to the plant.

2 In smaller pots the drainage material can be broken pieces of pot, known as crocks, or gravel.

Planting in Plastic

When buying plastic pots or boxes, check that the drainage holes are open. Some manufacturers mark the holes but leave it to the purchaser to punch or drill them out as required.

Plant Supports

Climbing plants in containers will need support. This can be provided by one or more canes which are pushed into the pot, a free-standing plant frame or a trellis fastened to a wall behind the container.

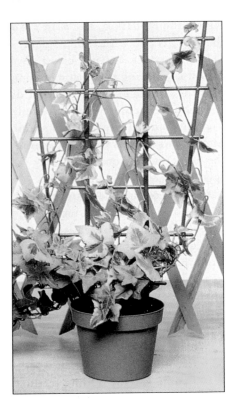

Planting in Wicker Baskets

If you wish to use a more unconventional container as a window box you may need to seal it with a sheet of plastic to prevent leakage.

1 Line the basket with a generous layer of moss which will prevent the compost leaking away.

2 Fill the basket with compost, and mix in plant food granules or any organic alternative you wish to use.

Saucers and Feet

Saucers are available for plastic and clay pots. They act as water reservoirs for the plants, and are used under houseplants to protect the surface they are standing on. Clay saucers must be fully glazed if they are used indoors or they will leave marks. Clay feet are available for terracotta pots. They will prevent the pot becoming waterlogged, but this also means that in a sunny position the pot will dry out very quickly and may need extra watering.

Plastic plant saucers can be used to line and protect containers which are not waterproof, such as this wooden apple-basket.

Hanging Gardens

When you want colour high up or relating closely to the building, the easiest way is to create a hanging garden, either in baskets or in wall-mounted containers. A purpose-made hanging basket is designed so that as the flowers grow, they cascade through the side and spill over the edge in a joyous show of colour, covering the whole basket. An alternative is to make the basket or container part of the display. Ordinary shopping baskets, buckets, agricultural containers, even kitchen equipment such as colanders, pots and pans, can be used.

Planting and Positioning Hanging Baskets

One hanging basket, alone on a wall, can look rather insignificant. Far better to plant up baskets in pairs, either with similar plants to create an echoing effect, or with clashing, contrasting colours. For a really stunning effect, entirely cover a wall with baskets, but remember that they are very demanding, and will need prolific watering in a dry mid-summer.

If the container is large and in danger of getting too heavy for its support, one trick is to put a layer of broken-up expanded polystyrene (from plant trays or electrical goods packaging) in the bottom of the container. This is lighter than the equivalent amount of compost and provides good drainage. Containers should have drainage holes, and baskets will need lining to stop the soil from being washed out while you are watering. Liners can be home-made from pieces of plastic sheet cut to size, with a layer of moss tucked between the basket and plastic for a more decorative look. Alternatively, you can use a proprietary liner, made from paper pulp, to fit purpose-made hanging baskets, or coconut matting – which comes in a variety of shapes and sizes to adapt to all kinds of baskets.

Whichever type of container you choose, it needs to be filled with a good compost, and adding fertilizer granules and water-retaining gel can also help promote lush results and make care and maintenance a little easier.

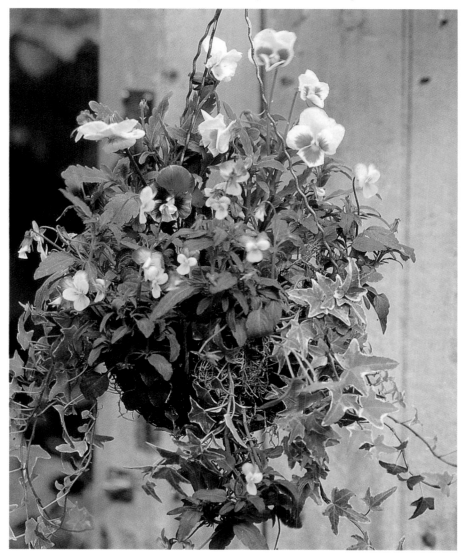

RIGHT: *Hanging baskets filled with pansies create a lovely focal point of gentle colour.*

Preparing Hanging Baskets

The key to successful hanging baskets is in the preparation. Time taken in preparing the basket for planting will be rewarded with a long-lasting colourful display. Slow-release plant food granules incorporated into the compost when planting ensure that the plants receive adequate nutrients throughout the growing season. It is essential to water hanging baskets every day, even in overcast weather, as they dry out very quickly. There are various ways to line a hanging basket.

Choosing a Lining

1 When buying a hanging basket, make sure that the chains are detachable. By unhooking one of the chains, they can be placed to one side of the basket, allowing you to work freely. Either rest the basket on a flat surface, or sit it on a flowerpot.

2 Traditionally, hanging baskets are lined with sphagnum moss. This looks very attractive and plants can be introduced at any point in the side of the basket. As sphagnum moss tends to dry out rather faster than other liners, it is advisable to use a compost containing water-retaining gel with this lining.

3 Coir fibre liners are a practical substitute for moss. Although not as good to look at, the coir will soon be hidden as the plants grow. The slits in the liner allow for planting in the side of the basket.

4 Cardboard liners are clean and easy to use. They are made in various sizes to fit most hanging baskets.

5 Press out the marked circles on the cardboard liner if you wish to plant into the side of the basket.

Underplanting a Hanging Basket

Underplanting helps to achieve a really lush-looking basket and soon conceals the shape of the container under flowers and foliage.

1 Line the lower half of the basket with a generous layer of moss.

2 Rest the rootball on the moss and gently guide the foliage through the side of the basket.

3 Add more moss to the basket, tucking it carefully around the plants to ensure that they are firmly in place. Add a further row of plants near the top edge of the basket, if required, and continue to line the basket with moss, finishing off with a collar of moss overlapping the rim of the basket. Fill with compost.

Colour Schemes for Containers

The artistry of container gardening lies in the way in which you arrange and combine all your raw materials: not just the plants themselves, but the container and the site you choose for it. Above all, sensitive colour co-ordination can make the difference between a planting scheme that is just pretty and one that draws gasps of admiration. The plants and the container need to enhance each other: lavender with blue violas in a stone urn, for instance, or fiery nasturtiums in terracotta pots. Think about the background, too – the colour of the surrounding walls, the paint on the window frame – and make the picture work as a whole.

Single-colour schemes can be striking, emphasizing the contrasting forms of the flowers and foliage, but so can strong contrasts of colour or tone. Let the glowing palette presented on the following pages inspire you to new heights of creativity.

ABOVE: *Pure white petunias and lobelia planted with a touch of grey foliage make a sophisticated display.*

A Silver and White Wall Basket

The helichrysum's silvery foliage and cool blue lavender flowers give a delicate colour scheme which would look good against a weathered background.

MATERIALS

30 cm (12 in) wall basket
Sphagnum moss
Compost
Slow-release plant food granules

PLANTS

2 lavenders (Lavandula dentata *var.* candicans)
Osteospermum *'Whirligig'*
2 Helichrysum petiolare

OSTEOSPERMUM

LAVENDER

HELICHRYSUM

GARDENER'S TIP

The lavender used in this project is fairly unusual – if you wish, you can substitute a low-growing variety such as 'Hidcote'.
Keep the helichrysum in check by pinching out its growing tips fairly regularly or it may take over the basket.

PLANT IN SPRING

1 Line the basket with moss and half-fill it with compost.

2 Mix in a half-teaspoon of plant food granules. Plant the lavenders in each corner.

3 Plant the osteospermum in the centre of the basket then add the helichrysums on either side.

4 Angle the plants to encourage them to trail over the side of the basket. Fill with compost. Water the basket and hang.

An All-white Window Box

A painted wooden window box filled with a white pelargonium, verbenas, marguerites, bacopa, and silver senecio is an ideal combination for a summer wedding celebration in the garden.

MATERIALS

45 cm (18 in) slatted wooden window box
Sphagnum moss
Compost
Slow-release plant food granules

PLANTS

White pelargonium
2 white marguerites (argyranthemums)
2 white trailing verbenas
2 Senecio cineraria 'Silver Dust'
White bacopa

SENECIO

BACOPA

PELARGONIUM

MARGUERITE

VERBENA

1 It is a good idea to line slatted wooden containers with moss before planting to prevent the compost from leaking out when the box is watered.

2 Fill the moss-lined window box with compost, mixing in 2 teaspoons of slow-release plant food granules. Plant the pelargonium in the centre of the window box towards the back.

3 Plant the marguerites on either side of the pelargonium.

4 Plant the trailing verbenas in the two back corners of the window box.

5 Plant the senecios in the front two corners of the window box to frame the bacopa.

6 Plant the bacopa centrally in the front of the box. Water the arrangement thoroughly and stand in a sunny position.

GARDENER'S TIP

To prolong the life of wooden containers it is advisable to empty them of compost before winter and store them under cover until spring.

PLANT IN LATE SPRING OR EARLY SUMMER

A Cascade of Lilac and Silver

Lilac petunias and violas are surrounded by a cascading curtain of variegated ground ivy and silver-leaved senecio in this softly coloured hanging basket.

MATERIALS

30 cm (12 in) hanging basket
Sphagnum moss
Compost
Slow-release plant food granules

PLANTS

3 deep blue violas
3 soft blue petunias
Variegated ground ivy (Glechoma hederacea *'Variegata'*)
3 Senecio cineraria 'Silver Dust'

SENECIO

IVY

PETUNIA

VIOLAS

GARDENER'S TIP

If the ground ivy becomes too rampant and threatens to throttle the other plants, prune it by removing some of the stems completely and reducing the length of the others.

PLANT IN LATE SPRING OR EARLY SUMMER

1 Line the lower half of the basket with moss. Plant the violas in the side by resting the rootballs on the moss, and carefully guiding the foliage between the wires. Line the rest of the basket with moss and fill with compost, mixing a teaspoon of slow-release plant food granules into the top layer.

2 Plant the three petunias, evenly spaced, in the top of the basket. Plant the ground ivy on one side to trail over the edge of the basket.

3 Plant the three senecios between the petunias. Water well and hang in a sunny position.

A Stencilled Purple Planter

This small stencilled wooden window box is full of blue flowers. In a particularly pretty mix, petunias are intertwined with brachycome daisies and trailing convolvulus. A pair of brackets hold it in place under the window.

MATERIALS

40 cm (16 in) wooden window box
Clay granules or other suitable drainage material
Compost
Slow-release plant food granules

PLANTS

3 blue petunias
2 blue brachycome daisies
Convolvulus sabatius

BRACHYCOME

PETUNIA

CONVOLVULUS

1 Line the base of the window box with clay granules or other suitable drainage material. Fill the window box with compost, mixing in a teaspoon of slow-release plant food granules.

2 Plant the three petunias, evenly spaced, towards the back of the box. Plant the brachycome daisies between the petunias.

3 Plant the convolvulus centrally at the front of the box. Water thoroughly and position in full or partial sun.

GARDENER'S TIP

If you are stencilling a wooden container for outside use, do not forget to seal the wood after decorating it. In this instance, a matt wood varnish in a light oak tint has been used.

PLANT IN LATE SPRING OR EARLY SUMMER

A Peachy Pink Wall Basket

The vivid flowers of the petunias and pelargonium contrast dramatically with the greeny-yellow lamiums. This basket is seen to best effect against a dark background.

MATERIALS

30 cm (12 in) wide wall basket
Sphagnum moss
Compost
Slow-release plant food granules

PLANTS

3 Lamium 'Golden Nuggets'
Peach/pink zonal Pelargonium
  'Palais', or similar
3 petunias

LAMIUM

PETUNIA

PELARGONIUM

1 Line the back and lower half of the front of the basket with moss. Plant the lamiums by resting the rootballs on the moss, and feeding the foliage through the side of the basket. Line the rest of the basket with moss.

2 Fill the basket with compost, mixing a half-teaspoon of slow-release plant food granules into the top layer. Plant the pelargonium in the centre of the basket against the back edge.

3 Plant one petunia in each corner and the third in front of the pelargonium. Water well and hang on a sunny wall.

GARDENER'S TIP

For a gentler colour scheme, the lamium can be replaced with the silver-grey foliage of *Helichrysum microphyllum*.

PLANT IN LATE SPRING OR EARLY SUMMER

Three Tiers of Colour

Scented petunias, delicate white marguerites and starry isotoma make a stunning layered arrangement. Use veined petunias, as they have the strongest scent.

MATERIALS

36 cm (14 in) terracotta window box
Crocks or other suitable drainage material
Compost
Slow-release plant food granules

PLANTS

2 white marguerites (argyranthemums)
3 petunias
3 isotoma

ISOTOMA

MARGUERITE

PETUNIA

GARDENER'S TIP

Try to position flowers where they can be seen at dusk, when their colours become far more intense and are a treat not to be missed.

PLANT IN LATE SPRING OR EARLY SUMMER

1 Cover the base of the window box with crocks. Fill with compost, mixing in 2 teaspoons of slow-release plant food granules.

2 Plant the marguerites on either side of the centre towards the back of the window box.

3 Plant one petunia in the centre and the other two at each end of the window box.

4 Plant the isotoma along the front edge of the window box. Water the arrangement well and stand in a sunny position.

Bright Splashes of Colour

MATERIALS

76 cm (30 in) plastic window
box with drainage holes
Compost
Slow-release plant food granules

PLANTS

2 yellow gazanias
3 Alaska nasturtiums
3 Brachycome 'Lemon Mist'
2 yellow snapdragons
(antirrhinums)

BRACHYCOME

NASTURTIUM

SNAPDRAGONS

GAZANIA

GARDENER'S TIP

Nasturtiums are among the easiest
plants to grow from seed.
Start them off about 4–6 weeks
before you plant your window box,
potting them on to keep them
growing vigorously.

PLANT IN THE SPRING

The leaves of the Alaska nasturtium look as if they have been splattered with cream paint. In this box they are planted with yellow-flowered snapdragons, gazanias and brachycome daisies.

1 Fill the window box with compost, mixing in 2 teaspoons of plant food. Plant the gazanias either side of the centre.

2 Plant the nasturtiums at either end and in the centre of the window box.

3 Plant the three brachycome plants, evenly spaced, along the front of the window box.

4 Plant the two snapdragons on either side of the central nasturtium. Water thoroughly and stand in a sunny position.

Summer Carnival

The orange markings on the throats of some of the mimulus flowers look wonderful with the orange-flowered pelargonium in this colourful basket. By the end of the season, trails of lysimachia leaves will form a waterfall of foliage around the base.

MATERIALS

36 cm (14 in) basket
Sphagnum moss
Compost
Slow-release plant food granules

PLANTS

Orange-flowered zonal
  pelargonium
3 Lysimachia nummularia 'Aurea'
3 mimulus

LYSIMACHIA

MIMULUS

PELARGONIUM

GARDENER'S TIP

Dead-head the flowers regularly
to encourage repeat flowering,
and if the mimulus start to
get leggy, cut back the offending
stems to a leaf joint.
New shoots will soon appear.

**PLANT IN LATE SPRING OR
EARLY SUMMER**

1 Line the basket with moss and fill it with compost, mixing a teaspoon of slow-release plant food granules into the top layer. Plant the pelargonium in the centre of the basket.

2 Plant the lysimachia, evenly spaced, around the edge of the basket, angling the plants so they will trail over the sides.

3 Plant the mimulus between the lysimachia. Water the hanging basket thoroughly and hang in a sunny spot.

A Sunny Wall Basket

MATERIALS

30 cm (12 in) wall basket
Sphagnum moss
Compost
Slow-release plant food granules

PLANTS

2 Lysimachia congestiflora
3 Alaska nasturtiums
3 mixed colour African marigolds
(tagetes)

LYSIMACHIA

NASTURTIUM

AFRICAN
MARIGOLDS

The vibrant yellows, oranges and reds of the flowers in this basket glow richly amongst the variegated leaves of the nasturtiums. As the season progresses the underplanted lysimachia will bear deep yellow flowers and add another layer of colour.

1 Line the back of the basket and half-way up the front with moss. Plant the lysimachia by resting the rootballs on the moss and feeding the foliage between the wires.

2 Line the rest of the basket and fill with compost, mixing in a half-teaspoon of plant food granules. Plant the nasturtiums along the back.

3 Plant the African marigolds in front of the nasturtiums. Water the basket well and hang it up in a sunny spot.

GARDENER'S TIP

If you have a large area of wall to cover, group two or three wall baskets together.
This looks very effective, especially when they are planted with the same plants.

PLANT IN SPRING

A Floral Chandelier

MATERIALS

36 cm (14 in) hanging basket
Sphagnum moss
Compost
Slow-release plant food granules

PLANTS

3 yellow lantanas, 2 variegated,
*   1 green-leaved*
2 Bidens ferulifolia
5 African marigolds (tagetes)

AFRICAN MARIGOLDS

LANTANA

BIDENS

The chandelier shape is a result of combining the spreading bidens with upright lantanas and marigolds. Since the variegated-leaf lantanas proved very slow to establish, a more vigorous green-leaved form was added later. As the season progresses, the strongly marked leaves of the variegated plants will become more dominant.

1 Line the basket with moss. Fill it with compost, mixing a teaspoon of slow-release plant food granules into the top layer. Plant the lantana in the centre.

2 Plant the two bidens opposite one another at the edge of the basket.

3 Plant the African marigolds around the lantana plants. Water thoroughly and hang in a sunny position.

GARDENER'S TIP

To complete the chandelier, make candle holders by twisting thick garden wire around
the base of yellow candles and add them to the hanging basket.

PLANT IN LATE SPRING OR EARLY SUMMER

Seasonal Planters

There's no need to confine your ideas to summer planting schemes, however exuberant. You can keep boxes and hanging baskets looking vibrant and beautiful all year round. It's a lovely reassurance that spring is on its way to see the earliest spring bulbs bursting into flower right outside your window, and judiciously planted pots can often be slipped into temporary gaps in the borders to bridge the seasons. One of the joys of container gardening is that you can put together combinations that will look their best in spring, summer or autumn, then swap them around to take centre stage at the appropriate time.

You may also have containers you don't want to move: if a stately classical urn is a focal point in your garden, give it all-year-round interest with an evergreen shrub or a beautifully clipped piece of topiary; you can ring seasonal changes by underplanting with spring and summer bedding plants.

ABOVE: *A colourful spring display underplanted with moss.*

Woodland Garden

You do not need your own woodland area for this garden, just a shady corner and an attractive container to hold a selection of plants that thrive in damp shade. The plants are buried in bark chippings in their pots and will relish these conditions as they closely imitate their natural habitat.

MATERIALS

50 cm (20 in) glazed pot
Bark chippings

FERNS

BLUEBELL

ANEMONE
BLANDA

PLANTS

Pot of bluebells
3 hardy ferns
Pot of Anemone blanda

1 Fill the container three-quarters full with bark chippings. Plant your largest pot (in this case the bluebells) first. Scoop a hollow in the bark and position the pot so that the base of the leaves is approximately 5 cm (2 in) below the rim of the container.

2 Cover the pot with bark so that the plastic is no longer visible and the plant is surrounded by chippings.

3 Arrange the ferns so that they relate attractively to one another. Fill the spaces between the ferns with bark.

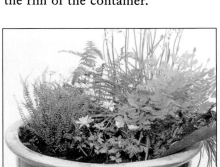

4 Add the *Anemone blanda* at the front of the container where its flowers will be seen to best advantage, and then top up the whole arrangement with bark. Stand the container in light shade and water.

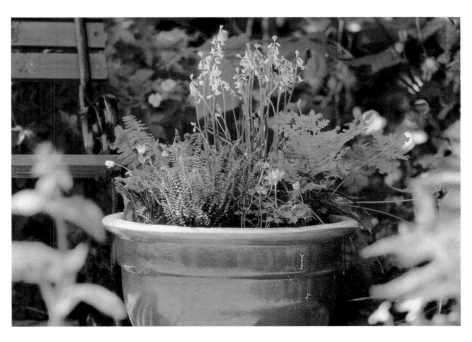

GARDENER'S TIP

After the bluebells and anemones have finished flowering, lift them out of the container in their pots and set them aside in a shady corner to rest. They can be replaced by other woodland plants such as wild strawberries or periwinkle.

PLANT IN EARLY SPRING

Display in a Copper Tub

A battered old washing boiler makes an attractive and characterful container for a display of white tulips, underplanted with purple violets and evergreen periwinkles.

MATERIALS

60 cm (24 in) copper boiler
20 cm (8 in) plastic pot
Compost

PLANTS

*20 white tulip bulbs
  or tulips in bud*
5 purple violets
*2 periwinkles
  (Vinca minor)*

VIOLET

TULIP

PERIWINKLE

GARDENER'S TIP

Lift the tulips when they have finished flowering and hang them up to dry in a cool airy place. They can be replanted late in autumn to flower again next year. Provided you pick off the dead heads, the violets will flower all summer. For a summer display, lift the central violet and plant a standard white marguerite in the centre of the container.

PLANT BULBS IN AUTUMN OR PLANTS IN BUD IN SPRING. PLANT THE VIOLETS AND PERIWINKLES IN SPRING

1 Place the upturned plastic pot in the base of the tub before filling it with compost. This will save on the amount of compost used, and will not have any effect on the growth of the plants as they will still have plenty of room for their roots.

2 If you are planting tulip bulbs, half-fill the container with compost, arrange the bulbs evenly over the surface and then cover them with a good 15 cm (6 in) of compost. This should be done in late autumn.

3 Do the underplanting in the early spring. The compost will have settled in the container and should be topped up to within 7.5 cm (3 in) of the rim. Remove the violets from their pots. Gently tweak the rootballs and loosen the roots to aid the plants' growth.

4 Plant one violet in the centre and four around the edges. Scoop out the soil by hand to avoid damaging the growing tips of the tulips beneath the surface.

5 Plant a periwinkle on either side of the central violet, again loosening the rootballs.

6 If you are planting tulips in bud, the whole scheme should be planted at the same time, interplanting the tulips with the violets and periwinkles. Position in sun or partial shade.

Spring Flowers in an Instant

An arrangement of pots of spring flowers is surrounded with bark to give the appearance of a planted window box. As soon as the flowers are over, the pots can be removed and left to die back, and the container is ready for its summer planting.

MATERIALS

40 cm (16 in) terracotta window box
Bark chippings

PLANTS

Pot of daffodils
Pot of yellow tulips
4 yellow pansies in pots

DAFFODIL

PANSY

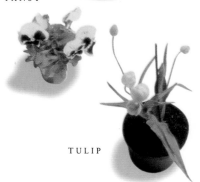

TULIP

GARDENER'S TIP

Once the flowers have finished and the pots have been removed from the window box, the pots of bulbs can be tucked away in a corner of the garden ready to flower again next year.

PLANT IN LATE WINTER OR EARLY SPRING

1 Position the pot of daffodils at the right-hand end of the window box.

2 Position the pot of tulips at the left-hand end of the window box.

3 Fill the centre and around the pots with bark chippings until the window box is half-full.

4 Position the pansies between the tulips and the daffodils, and add bark until all the pots are concealed. Water moderately and stand in any position.

Layers of Flowers

LOBELIAS

TOBACCO

PELARGONIUM

BUSY LIZZIE

MATERIALS

36 cm (14 in) fibre window box
Drainage material
Compost
Slow-release plant food granules

PLANTS

2 white tobacco plants
Variegated Pelargonium
  'l'Elégante'
2 pink busy Lizzies (impatiens)
3 white lobelias

This window box is unusual as the colours are in distinct layers, with upright white flowering tobacco above pink busy Lizzies, and tumbling white variegated pelargonium and lobelias. The fibre window box is concealed by a decorative twig container.

1 Put some drainage material in the base of the window box; fill with compost, mixing in 2 teaspoons of plant food granules. Plant the flowering tobacco near the back edge.

2 Plant the pelargonium at the front of the window box, in the centre.

3 Plant the busy Lizzies at each end of the window box.

4 Plant one of the lobelias between the flowering tobacco, and the other two on either side of the pelargonium.

GARDENER'S TIP

Somehow, rogue blue lobelias have appeared among the white plants. This sort of thing often happens in gardening and, as in this case, the accidental addition can turn out well.

PLANT IN SPRING

A Miniature Cottage Garden

This basket derives its charm from its simple planting scheme. Pot marigolds and parsley are planted with bright blue felicias to create a basket which would look at home on the wall of a cottage or outside the kitchen door.

FELICIA

PARSLEY

POT MARIGOLDS

MATERIALS

36 cm (14 in) hanging basket
Sphagnum moss
Compost
Slow-release plant food granules

PLANTS

5 parsley plants
3 pot marigolds (Calendula 'Gitana', or similar)
3 felicias

1 Line the lower half of the basket with moss.

2 Plant the parsley into the sides of the basket by resting the rootballs on the moss, and gently feeding the foliage through the wires.

3 Line the rest of the basket with moss, carefully tucking it around the roots of the parsley.

4 Fill the basket with compost, mixing a teaspoon of slow-release plant food granules into the top layer.

5 Plant the three pot marigolds, evenly spaced, in the top of the basket.

6 Plant the felicias between the marigolds. Water well and hang in full or partial sun.

GARDENER'S TIP

Regular dead-heading will keep the basket looking good, but allow at least one of the marigold flowers to form a seedhead and you will be able to grow your own plants next year.

PLANT IN SPRING

Full of Cheer

Vivid red pelargoniums and
verbenas are combined with
cheerful yellow bidens and soft
green helichrysums in this
planter, which brightens the
exterior of an old barn.

MATERIALS

*76 cm (30 in) plastic window
box*
Compost
Slow-release plant food granules

PLANTS

3 scarlet pelargoniums
2 Bidens ferulifolia
2 red trailing verbenas
2 Helichrysum petiolare 'Aureum'

HELICHRYSUM

VERBENA

PELARGONIUM

BIDENS

GARDENER'S TIP

Regular dead-heading and an occasional
foliar feed will keep the pelargoniums
flowering prolifically all summer.

PLANT IN SPRING

1 The easiest way to open the drainage holes in a plastic planter is with an electric drill.

2 Fill the window box with compost, mixing in 2 teaspoons of slow-release plant food granules.

3 Plant the pelargoniums, evenly spaced, in the window box.

4 Plant the two bidens on either side of the central pelargonium to spill over the front of the planter.

5 Plant the two verbenas on either side of the central pelargonium towards the back of the planter.

6 Plant the helichrysums in the front corners. Water thoroughly and stand the box in a sunny position.

Hot Flowers in a Cool Container

Shocking-pink petunias and verbenas are the dominant plants in this window box which also features a softer pink marguerite and silver helichrysum. The dark green of the wooden window box is a pleasing foil for the vibrant flowers.

MATERIALS

76 cm (30 in) plastic window box with drainage holes
90 cm (3 ft) wooden window box (optional)
Compost
Slow-release plant food granules

PLANTS

Trailing pink marguerite (Argyranthemum 'Flamingo')
2 bright pink verbenas, such as 'Sissinghurst'
3 shocking-pink petunias
4 Helichrysum petiolare microphyllum

MARGUERITE

VERBENA

PETUNIA

HELICHRYSUM

GARDENER'S TIP

To add height to this scheme, buy some 30 cm (12 in) green plant sticks. Push two into the soil behind each of the verbenas, and train them upwards.

PLANT IN LATE SPRING OR EARLY SUMMER

1 Fill the plastic window box with compost, mixing in 3 teaspoons of slow-release plant food granules. Plant the marguerite centre front.

2 Plant the verbenas in the back corners of the window box.

3 Plant one of the petunias behind the marguerite, and the other two on either side of it.

4 Plant one helichrysum on each side of the central petunia, and the other two in the front corners of the window box. Water well and lift into place. Stand in a sunny position.

Pot of Sunflowers

Sunflowers grow very well in pots provided you are not growing the giant varieties. Grow your own from seed; there are many kinds to choose from, including the one with double flowers used here.

MATERIALS

30 cm (12 in) glazed pot
Polystyrene or similar
  drainage material
Equal mix loam-based compost
  and container compost
Slow-release plant
  food granules

PLANTS

3 strong sunflower seedlings,
approximately 20 cm (8 in) tall

SUNFLOWER
SEEDLING

GARDENER'S TIP

Allow at least one of the sunflower heads to set seed. As the plant starts to die back, cut off the seedhead and hang it upside-down to ripen. Reserve some seeds for next year and then hang the seedhead outside for the birds.

PLANT SEEDS IN SPRING
AND SEEDLINGS IN SUMMER TO
FLOWER IN LATE SUMMER

1 Line the base of the pot with drainage material and fill with the compost mix. Scoop out evenly spaced holes for each seedling and plant, firming the compost around the plants.

2 Scatter 1 tablespoon of plant food granules on the surface of the compost. Place in a sunny position, out of the wind, and water regularly.

Evergreens with Extra Colour

They may be easy to look after but all-year-round window boxes can start to look a bit lifeless after a couple of seasons. It does not take much trouble to add a few seasonal flowers and it makes all the difference to a display.

MATERIALS

76 cm (30 in) plastic window box
Compost
Slow-release plant food granules

PLANTS

Hebe *'Baby Marie'*
Convolvulus cneorum
Potentilla *'Nunk'*
Variegated ivies
2 Diascia *'Ruby Field'*
Pink marguerite (Argyranthemum *'Flamingo'*)

IVY

CONVOLVULUS

POTENTILLA

MARGUERITE

DIASCIA

HEBE

1 Check the drainage holes are open in the base and, if not, drill or punch them open. Fill the window box with compost, mixing in 3 teaspoons of slow-release plant food granules. Plant the hebe in the centre.

2 Plant the convolvulus near one end of the window box.

3 Plant the potentilla near the other end of the window box.

4 Plant the two ivies at the front corners of the window box.

5 Plant the diascias on either side of the hebe at the front of the window box.

6 Plant the marguerite between the hebe and the convolvulus at the back. Water well and stand in full or partial sun.

GARDENER'S TIP

At the end of the summer, remove the diascias and marguerite, feed the remaining plants with more granules, and fill the spaces with winter-flowering plants such as pansies or heathers.

PLANT IN SPRING

Classic Winter Colours

Convolvulus cneorum is an attractive small shrub with eye-catching silver-grey leaves, which last through winter, and white flowers in spring and summer. Planted with ice-blue pansies, it makes a softly subtle display from autumn to spring.

MATERIALS

30 cm (12 in) hanging basket
Sphagnum moss
Compost

PLANTS

8 silver/blue pansies (Viola
  'Silver Wings', or similar)
Convolvulus cneorum

CONVOLVULUS

PANSIES

1 Half-line the basket with moss and fill with compost to the top of the moss. Plant four of the pansies into the side of the basket by placing their rootballs on the compost, and gently guiding the leaves through the side of the basket.

2 Line the rest of the basket with moss and top up with compost. Plant the convolvulus in the centre of the basket.

3 Plant the remaining four pansies around the convolvulus. Water well and hang in sun or partial shade.

GARDENER'S TIP

At the end of the winter cut back any dead wood or straggly branches on the *Convolvulus cneorum*, and give a liquid feed to encourage new growth. Small shrubs such as this may be used in hanging baskets for one season, but will then need planting into a larger container or the border.

PLANT IN AUTUMN

An Evergreen Wall Basket

Pansies will flower throughout the winter. Even if they are flattened by rain, frost or snow, at the first sign of improvement in the weather their heads will pop up again to bring brightness to the dullest day. They have been planted with ivies to provide colour from early autumn through to late spring.

MATERIALS

30 cm (12 in) wall basket
Sphagnum moss
Compost

PLANTS

2 golden variegated ivies
2 copper pansies (viola)
Yellow pansy (viola)

PANSIES

IVY

GARDENER'S TIP

Winter baskets do not need regular feeding and should only be watered in very dry conditions. To prolong the flowering life of the pansies, dead-head regularly and pinch out any straggly stems to encourage new shoots from the base.

PLANT IN AUTUMN

1 Line the basket with moss. Three-quarters fill the basket with compost and position the ivies with their rootballs resting on the compost. Guide the stems through the sides of the basket so that they trail downwards. Pack more moss around the ivies and top up the basket with compost.

2 Plant the two copper pansies at either end of the basket.

3 Plant the yellow pansy in the centre. Water well and hang in shade or semi-shade.

Edible Collections

*What could be nicer than reaching out of the kitchen window to gather fresh herbs
from the window-sill, or eating succulent tomatoes or strawberries grown on
the balcony? If you don't have room for a vegetable patch, even if you don't have
a garden at all, you can still enjoy home-grown produce if you plant it in containers.
Go for compact varieties of beans and tomatoes, and choose lettuces such as
'Salad Bowl' so that you can pick just what you need and leave the plants to go on
growing. Alpine strawberries are both decorative and delicious tumbling out of a
hanging basket, and you can grow herbs for their looks as well as their flavour, choosing
variegated mints, red-leaved basil or purple sage to contribute to the visual feast.*

ABOVE: *Herbs thrive on a sunny windowsill.*

Herbs in the Shade

Although the Mediterranean herbs need lots of sunshine, there are many others which prefer a cooler situation to look and taste their best. This window box, ideal for just outside the kitchen door or window, has an interesting variety of mints, sorrel, chives, lemon balm and parsley.

MATERIALS

50 cm (20 in) terracotta window box
Polystyrene or other suitable drainage material
Compost
Slow-release plant food granules, pelleted chicken manure, or similar organic plant food

PLANTS

Lemon balm
3 mints (black peppermint, silver mint and curly spearmint were used here)
Sorrel
Chives
Parsley

LEMON BALM

MINTS

CHIVE

SORREL

PARSLEY

MINT

1 Line the base of the container with polystyrene or similar drainage material. Top up with compost, mixing in 3 teaspoons of slow-release plant food granules or organic alternative.

2 Plant the lemon balm and two of the mints along the back of the window box.

3 Plant the third mint, the sorrel and the chives along the front. Finally, plant the parsley in the centre. Position the box in light shade and water thoroughly.

GARDENER'S TIP

Use the freshly picked mint to make refreshing teas. Pour hot boiled water over a few washed leaves and infuse for five minutes.

PLANT IN EARLY SPRING

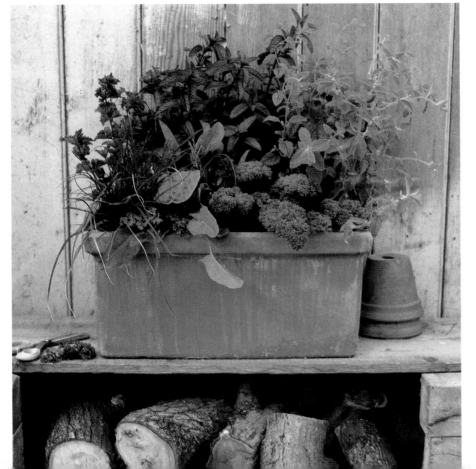

Vital Ingredients

A lovely present for an enthusiastic cook, this window box contains chervil, coriander, fennel, garlic, purple sage, French tarragon, savory, origanum and basil.

MATERIALS

45 cm (18 in) wooden window box
Crocks or other suitable drainage material
Compost
Slow-release plant food granules, pelleted chicken manure, or similar organic plant food

PLANTS

French tarragon
Chervil
Garlic
Coriander
Purple sage
Basil
Fennel
Savory
Origanum

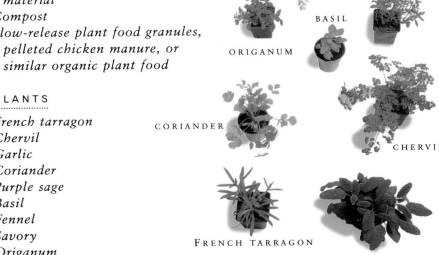

FENNEL   GARLIC

SAVORY

BASIL

ORIGANUM

CORIANDER

CHERVIL

FRENCH TARRAGON

PURPLE SAGE

GARDENER'S TIP

There are now various kinds of basil seed available (some specialists sell at least 12), with varieties ranging from Greek to Indonesian. The key point when growing them is to remove the flower buds the moment they appear as the leaves will quickly lose their flavour once the flowers open.

PLANT IN SPRING

1 Line the base of the container with crocks or other suitable drainage material. Fill the window box with compost, mixing in a teaspoon of slow-release plant food granules or an organic alternative.

2 Before planting the herbs, arrange them in the window box in their pots.

3 Plant the back row of herbs in the window box first.

4 Plant more herbs at the front of the window box. Water well and stand in a sunny position.

Wine Case Herb Garden

Add a coat of varnish to an old wine case to make an attractive and durable container for a miniature herb garden. The container can be placed near the kitchen door or on a balcony.

MATERIALS

Wooden wine case
Pliers
Sandpaper
Paintbrush
Light oak semi-matt varnish
Crocks or similar drainage material
Compost with 1/3 added coarse grit
Slow-release plant food granules or pelleted chicken manure
Bark chippings

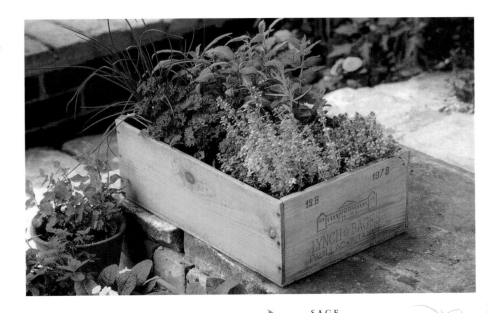

PLANTS

Selection of 7 herbs, such as sage, chives, parsley, mint, tarragon, lemon thyme and creeping thyme

SAGE

PARSLEY

CHIVES

GARDENER'S TIP

Some herbs like cool, partial shade while others like hot, dry, free-draining soil. A mixed herb garden will thrive for only one growing season.

PLANT IN SPRING

1 Remove any wire staples from around the edges of the box and sand down the rough edges. Apply two coats of varnish on the inside and outside of the box, allowing the varnish to dry thoroughly between coats. When dry, cover the base of the box with a layer of crocks or similar drainage material.

2 Before planting, decide how you are going to arrange the plants in the container to achieve a pleasing balance of colour, height and shape.

3 Fill the box with gritty compost and plant from one end of the box to the other. Loosen the rootballs, as this will help the plants to root into the surrounding compost.

4 When the planting is complete, scatter 2 tablespoons of plant food granules or pelleted chicken manure on the surface of the compost. Firm in the plants and mulch with bark chippings to retain moisture. Water well.

Home-grown Salads

These compact but heavy-fruiting tomato plants have been specially bred to be grown in containers. Teamed with lettuce, radishes, chives and parsley, they provide all the ingredients for a fresh garden salad.

GARDENER'S TIP

Keep the tomato plants watered at all times, and liquid feed with a proprietary tomato food or liquid seaweed fertilizer.

PLANT IN SPRING

MATERIALS

76 cm (30 in) plastic window box
Compost
Slow-release plant food granules, pelleted chicken manure or similar organic plant food

PLANTS

3 'Tumbler' tomatoes
Chives
4 lettuces, 'Little Gem' or 'Corsair'
2 'Salad Bowl' lettuces
4 parsley plants
Radish seed

TOMATO

LETTUCE

CHIVES

LETTUCE

PARSLEY

1 Check the drainage holes are open in the base of the window box and, if not, drill or punch them open. Fill with compost, mixing in 2 teaspoons of slow-release plant food granules or organic alternative. Plant the tomatoes, evenly spaced, along the centre.

2 Plant the chives in front of the middle tomato plant. Plant the 'Little Gem' or 'Corsair' lettuces diagonally to one another between the tomato plants.

3 Plant the 'Salad Bowl' lettuces in the front corners. Plant the parsley plants diagonally opposite one another alongside the 'Little Gem' or 'Corsair' lettuces.

4 Scatter radish seed between the plants and gently rake into the soil. Water thoroughly and stand in a sunny position.

Wild Strawberry Basket

Wild strawberries can be grown in a basket and enjoyed anywhere, whether in the countryside or a small city garden.

MATERIALS

30 cm (12 in) square wire basket
Sphagnum moss
Equal mix loam-based compost and container compost
Slow-release plant food granules or organic plant food

PLANTS

4 alpine strawberry plants

ALPINE STRAWBERRY

1 Line the base and sides of the basket with a generous layer of sphagnum moss.

2 Fill the lined area with compost. Scoop out a hollow for each strawberry plant, and press the compost firmly around the rootball as you plant.

3 Scatter a tablespoon of plant food granules on the surface of the compost.

4 Tuck more moss around the edges and under the leaves to conserve moisture and stop the fruit touching the soil. Water and place in full or partial sun.

GARDENER'S TIP

Propagate strawberry runners by pinning the plantlets into small pots of compost. A loop of wire or a hairpin placed on either side of the plantlet will hold it firmly in place until it has rooted. Then simply cut the runner and you have a new strawberry plant.

PLANT IN SPRING TO FRUIT IN SUMMER

The Good Life

This window box will not exactly make you self-sufficient, but it is surprising how many different vegetables can be grown in a small space. It is perfect for anyone who likes the taste of home-grown vegetables but does not have a garden to grow them in.

MATERIALS

76 cm (30 in) plastic window box
Compost
Slow-release plant food granules, pelleted chicken manure or similar organic plant food

PLANTS

Garlic
3 Chinese leaves
4 plugs of beetroot (see Gardener's Tip)
Pepper plant
3 dwarf French beans
3 plugs of shallots

BEETROOT   CHINESE LEAVES

GARLIC

FRENCH BEAN

PEPPER

SHALLOTS

1 Check the drainage holes are open in the container's base. Fill the window box with compost, mixing in 2 teaspoons of slow-release plant food granules or an organic alternative. Start planting from one end.

2 Starting at the right-hand end of the window box, first plant the garlic. Next plant the Chinese leaves.

3 Follow these with the plugs of beetroot.

4 Plant the pepper plant next, just to the left of the centre.

5 Now plant the three dwarf French bean plants.

6 Finally, plant the shallot plugs in the left-hand corner. Water well and stand in full or partial sun.

GARDENER'S TIP

It is now possible to buy plugs of small vegetable plants at garden centres. There is no need to separate the plants provided there is sufficient room between the clumps.

PLANT IN SPRING

A Taste for Flowers

It is often said that something "looks good enough to eat", and in this instance it is true. All the flowers in this window box may be used for flavour and garnishes.

MATERIALS

*36 cm (14 in) terracotta window
    box*
*Crocks or other suitable drainage
    material*
Compost
*Slow-release plant food granules,
    pelleted chicken manure or
    similar organic plant food*

PLANTS

Chives
2 nasturtiums
*2 pansies (viola) with well-
    marked "faces"*
2 pot marigolds (calendula)

CHIVE

NASTURTIUM

PANSY

MARIGOLDS

GARDENER'S TIP

To keep all the plants producing
flowers, dead-head regularly.
Once a plant has set seed it
considers its work done and will
produce fewer and fewer flowers.

PLANT IN EARLY SPRING

1 Cover the base of the window box with a layer of crocks or similar drainage material. Fill with compost, mixing in 2 teaspoons of slow-release plant food granules or an organic alternative. Plant the chives in the right-hand corner.

2 Plant one of the nasturtiums in the left-hand corner and the other centre-front.

3 Plant one pansy at the back next to the chives, and the other at the front to the left of the central nasturtium.

4 Plant one of the marigolds at the back between the pansy and nasturtium, and the other one just behind the central nasturtium.

Beans and Parsley in a Basket

A hanging basket planted with dwarf beans and parsley can be surprisingly productive and will outwit all but the most acrobatic of snails.

MATERIALS

36 cm (14 in) hanging basket
Sphagnum moss
Compost
Slow-release plant food granules

PLANTS

7 parsley plants
3 dwarf bean plants

DWARF BEAN

PARSLEY

1 Line the lower half of the basket with moss and half-fill with compost.

2 Plant the parsley into the sides of the basket, resting the root-balls on the compost and feeding the leaves through the wires.

3 Gently separate the bean plants from one another.

4 Line the upper half of the basket with moss and add more compost. Mix a teaspoon of slow-release plant food granules into the top layer. Plant the beans in the compost. Water the basket thoroughly and hang in partial sun.

GARDENER'S TIP

Fruit and vegetable hanging baskets need quite a lot of attention to crop well. They should be kept moist at all times and need a liquid feed once a week. If you are going to be away, move the basket into the shade, where it will not dry out so quickly.

PLANT IN SPRING

Good Enough to Eat

All the plants in this basket bear an edible crop: the tomato fruit, nasturtium flowers and parsley leaves. You could even impress your family or guests with a "hanging basket salad", using all three together.

MATERIALS

36 cm (14 in) hanging basket
Sphagnum moss
Compost
Slow-release plant food granules

PLANTS

6 parsley plants
3 trailing nasturtiums
3 'Tumbler' tomatoes, or similar

PARSLEY

TRAILING NASTURTIUM

TOMATO

GARDENER'S TIP

If you would prefer to grow your plants organically, plant this basket using an organic compost and use natural plant foods such as pelleted chicken manure or a liquid seaweed feed.

PLANT IN LATE SPRING OR EARLY SUMMER

1 Line the lower half of the basket with moss.

2 Plant three parsley plants into the side of the basket by resting the rootballs on the moss, and feeding the leaves through the side of the basket.

3 Line the basket to just below the rim and fill with compost. Mix a teaspoon of slow-release plant food granules into the top of the compost. Plant three nasturtium plants into the side of the basket, just below the rim.

4 Finish lining the basket with moss, being careful to tuck plenty of moss around the nasturtiums.

5 Plant the tomato plants in the top of the basket.

6 Plant the remaining three parsley plants amongst the tomatoes in the top of the basket. Water well and hang in a sunny position. Liquid feed regularly.

Scented Collections

Scent gives a lovely extra dimension to container planting schemes, especially for planters that are sited at "nose" level, such as window boxes. On warm days the aromas will drift in through open windows. Use plants with scented leaves for a really lasting effect: herbs such as lavender and mint are invaluable foils for larger-flowered plants and will fill the air with fragrance. The scented-leaf pelargoniums are perfect container plants and you can choose from a wide variety of lovely variegations and leaf shapes as well as perfumes that range from lemon and mint to rose. Their charming pink flowers are an added bonus. Put scented plants in containers near paths and doorways, where their rich fragrances will be released each time you brush past them. A fragrant plant in a pot by the front door makes a special welcome for visitors.

ABOVE: *Lavender is always a favourite for its delightful scent. Here it is combined with scaevolas and trailing convolvulus.*

Sweet-smelling Summer Flowers

Scented pelargonium and verbena are combined with heliotrope and petunias to make a window box that is fragrant as well as a visual pleasure.

MATERIALS

40cm (16 in) terracotta window box
Crocks or other suitable drainage material
Compost
Slow-release plant food granules

PLANTS

Scented-leaf Pelargonium 'Lady Plymouth'
3 soft pink petunias
Heliotrope
2 Verbena 'Pink Parfait'

HELIOTROPE

PETUNIA

VERBENA

PELARGONIUM

GARDENER'S TIP

At the end of the summer the pelargonium can be potted up and kept through the winter as a houseplant. Reduce the height of the plant by at least a half and it will soon send out new shoots.

PLANT IN LATE SPRING OR EARLY SUMMER

1 Cover the base of the window box with a layer of crocks. Fill with compost, mixing in 2 teaspoons of slow-release plant food granules. Plant the pelargonium to the right of centre, towards the back of the window box.

2 Plant a petunia in each corner and one in the centre at the front of the window box.

3 Plant the heliotrope to the left of the pelargonium.

4 Plant one verbena behind the heliotrope and the other in front of the pelargonium. Water well and place in a sunny position.

Sweet-scented Lavender

In this large basket an unusual lavender is planted amongst *Convolvulus sabatius* and the fan-shaped flowers of scaevola in cool, toning shades of blue. Underplanting with trailing plants ensures that the flowers cascade down the sides of the basket.

MATERIALS

40 cm (16 in) hanging basket
Sphagnum moss
Compost
Slow-release plant food granules

PLANTS

3 Convolvulus sabatius
2 *scaevolas*
2 *lavenders* (Lavandula dentata *var.* candicans)

LAVENDER

CONVOLVULUS

SCAEVOLA

1 Line the lower half of the basket with moss.

2 Plant two of the convolvulus into the side of the basket by resting the rootballs on the moss, and carefully guiding the foliage between the wires.

3 Plant one of the scaevolas into the side of the basket in the same way.

4 Line the rest of the basket with moss, taking care to tuck it around the underplanting.

5 Fill the basket with compost, mixing a teaspoon of slow-release plant food granules into the top layer. Plant the lavenders opposite one another in the top.

6 Plant the remaining convolvulus and scaevola plants in the spaces between the lavenders. Water thoroughly and hang in a sunny position.

GARDENER'S TIP

If you are unable to obtain *Lavandula dentata*, the varieties called 'Hidcote' or 'Munstead' are readily available and make suitable substitutes.

PLANT IN SPRING

Scented Window Box

The soft silvers and blues of the flowers and foliage beautifully complement this verdigris window box. The scent of the lavender and petunias will drift magically through open windows.

MATERIALS

60 cm (24 in) window box
Gravel or similar drainage material
Equal mix loam-based compost and container compost
Slow-release plant food granules

PLANTS

2 lavenders
2 pale blue petunias
4 deep blue petunias
4 Chaenorhinum glareosum (or lilac lobelia)
6 Helichrysum petiolare

PETUNIA

CHAENORHINUM

LAVENDER

HELICHRYSUM

GARDENER'S TIP

To keep a densely planted container like this looking its best it is necessary to feed regularly with a liquid feed, or more simply to mix slow-release plant food granules into the surface of the compost to last the whole summer. Cut back the lavender heads after flowering to ensure bushy flowering plants again next year.

PLANT IN LATE SPRING OR EARLY SUMMER

1 Fill the bottom 5 cm (2 in) of the window box with drainage material and half-fill with compost. Position the lavender plants, loosening the soil around the roots before planting, as they will establish better this way.

2 Now arrange the flowering plants around the lavender, leaving spaces for the helichrysums between them.

3 Finally, add the helichrysums and fill between the plants with compost, pressing firmly so that no air gaps are left around the roots. Place in a sunny position and water regularly.

A Butterfly Garden

We should all do our bit to encourage butterflies into our gardens and this window box filled with sedum, marjoram, thyme and origanum should prove irresistible. All these plants are perennials and can be over-wintered in the window box.

MATERIALS

60 cm (24 in) stone window box
Crocks or other suitable drainage
  material
Compost
Slow-release plant food granules

PLANTS

Sedum *'Ruby Glow'*
Marjoram
*Lemon thyme (*Thymus
  citriodorus*)*
*Common thyme (*Thymus
  vulgaris*)*
Origanum

LEMON
THYME

ORIGANUM

MARJORAM

COMMON
THYME

SEDUM

GARDENER'S TIP

You can imitate the look of an old stone window box by painting a new one with a dilute mixture of liquid seaweed plant food and water. This encourages moss to grow and ages the stone.

PLANT IN SPRING

1 Cover the base of the window box with a layer of crocks or other suitable drainage material. Fill with compost, mixing in 3 teaspoons of slow-release plant food granules.

2 Plant the sedum off-centre to the left of the window box and the marjoram to the left of the sedum.

3 Plant the lemon thyme in the centre front and the common thyme in the back right-hand corner of the container.

4 Plant the origanum in the front right-hand corner of the window box. Water well and place in a sunny position.

Scented Spring Planter

Lilies-of-the-valley grow very well in containers and they will thrive in the shade where their delicate scented flowers stand out amongst the greenery. Surrounding the plants with bun moss is practical as well as attractive as it will stop the soil splashing back on to the leaves and flowers during fierce spring showers.

MATERIALS

Tinware planter
Clay granules
Compost
Bun moss

PLANTS

6–8 pots of lily-of-the-valley

LILY OF THE
VALLEY

1 Fill the bottom of the planter with 5 cm (2 in) of clay granules to improve drainage.

2 Cover the granules with a layer of compost and arrange the lily-of-the-valley plants evenly on the compost.

3 Fill in around the plants with more compost, making sure to press firmly around the plants so that they won't rock about in the wind. Now cover the compost with bun moss, fitting it snugly around the stems of the lily-of-the-valley, as this will also help keep the plants upright.

GARDENER'S TIP

If you want to bring your planter indoors to enjoy the scent of the flowers, use a container without drainage holes in the base, but be very careful not to overwater. Once the plants have finished flowering replant them in a pot with normal drainage holes or in the garden. They are woodland plants and will be quite happy under trees.

PLANT IN EARLY SPRING

A Nose-twitcher Window Box

One of the French country names for the nasturtium means 'nose-twitcher' and refers to the peppery smell of the plant. It has been planted here with the equally aromatic and colourful ginger mint and pot marigold.

MATERIALS

25 cm (10 in) terracotta window box
Crocks or other suitable drainage material
Compost
Slow-release plant food granules

PLANTS

Variegated ginger mint
Nasturtium, Tropaeolum *'Empress of India',*
* or similar*
Pot marigold (Calendula 'Gitana', or similar)

MARIGOLD

NASTURTIUM

GINGER
MINT

1 Cover the base of the window box with a layer of crocks or similar drainage material. Fill the container with compost, mixing in a half-teaspoon of slow-release plant food granules.

2 Plant the ginger mint on the right of the container.

3 Plant the nasturtium in the centre.

4 Plant the marigold on the left of the container. Water well and stand in full or partial sun.

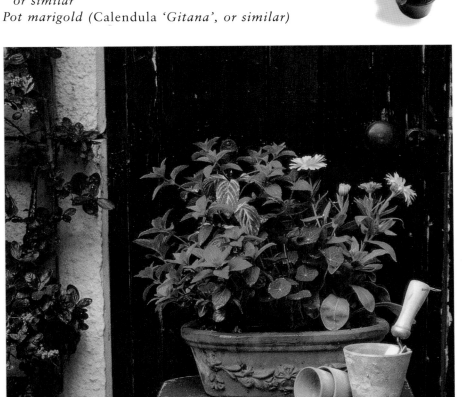

GARDENER'S TIP

A small window box like this one can double as a table-centre for an outdoor meal.

PLANT IN SPRING

Star-jasmine in a Villandry Planter

The soft, seductive scent of the star-jasmine makes this a perfect container to place by the side of a door where the scent will be appreciated by all who pass through.

STAR-
JASMINE

MATERIALS

50 cm (20 in) villandry planter or similar, preferably self-watering
Equal mix loam-based compost and standard compost
Slow-release plant food granules
Bark chippings

PLANTS

*Star-jasmine (*Trachelospermum jasminoides*)*

GARDENER'S TIP

Use a plastic liner inside all large planters. It is easier to remove the liner when replanting rather than dismantle the entire container.

PLANT IN LATE SPRING OR EARLY SUMMER

1 Feed the wicks through the holes in the base of the liner.

2 Fill the water reservoir in the base of the planter to the top of the overflow pipe, and place the liner inside the planter.

3 Fill the bottom of the liner with compost while pulling through the wicks so that they reach the level of the roots.

4 Remove the jasmine from its pot, gently tease the roots loose and stand it in the planter.

NOTE *Steps 1–3 are for self-watering planters only.*

5 Add compost and firm it around the rootball of the jasmine. Scatter 2 tablespoons of plant food granules on the surface, and gently work them into the top layer of compost with the trowel.

6 Mulch around the plant with a layer of bark chippings, then water. Check the reservoir of the self-watering container once a week and top up if necessary. Conventional pots should be watered daily in the early morning or evening during hot weather.

The Young
Container Gardener

Most children become enthusiastic gardeners as soon as they have a patch of soil they can really call their own, and this applies equally to containers. What is more, if they can make or decorate their container before planting it up, they'll get a real sense of achievement. These projects use easily available plants and seeds that can be bought with pocket money and are reliable and free-flowering, given a little care and attention. There are suggestions for easy-to-grow vegetables and a small pond made from a toy-box that will quickly become a haven for wildlife. Youngsters will have every reason to be proud of the results.

ABOVE: *An old pair of boots can make a fun container for brightly coloured flowers.*

Cactus Garden

Planting a bowl of cacti may take a little care and patience, but it is worth the effort since children love cacti. Once planted, the cacti ask nothing more than benevolent neglect.

MATERIALS

25 cm (10 in) terracotta bowl
Cactus compost
Newspaper
Cactus gravel

PLANTS

Euphorbia submammilaris
Rebutia muscula
Rose pincushion (Mammilaria zeilmanniana)
Cheiridopsis candidissima
Astrophytum ornatum
Prickly pear (Opuntia)

REBUTIA   EUPHORBIA   PRICKLY
                                    PEAR

CHEIRIDOPSIS

ASTROPHYTUM

ROSE PINCUSHION

GARDENER'S TIP

If there are young children in your household be sure to choose the site of your cactus garden with care. If cacti are too aggressive for you, plant succulents instead: they require the same treatment, but are free of thorns.

PLANT AT ANY TIME OF THE YEAR

1 Fill the bowl with cactus compost to within 5 cm (2 in) of the rim. Prepare a thickly folded strip of newspaper to help you handle the cacti.

2 Before planting, decide on your arrangement of the plants by standing them, in their pots, in the bowl.

3 Ease the plants from their pots, surround them with a newspaper collar and lift into place. Handle more ferocious plants carefully, and leave the really prickly cacti until last or you will stab yourself on them as you are planting the rest.

4 Fill in around the plants with extra compost if needed. Add a finishing touch with a top-dressing of fine cactus gravel. Stand in good light and water sparingly.

Blooming Old Boots

This is a blooming wonderful way to recycle an old pair of boots, the bigger the better. It just goes to show that almost anything can be used to grow plants in, as long as it has a few holes in the bottom for drainage. Try an old football, a sports bag, or even an old hat for plant containers with lots of character.

BEDDING PLANTS

MATERIALS

Knife
Old pair of working boots
Compost

PLANTS

Selection of bedding plants such as impatiens, pelargoniums, verbenas, pansies and lobelias

1 Using a knife very carefully, make some holes in between the stitching of the sole for drainage. It helps if there are holes there already.

2 Fill the boots with compost, pushing it down right to the toe so there are no air spaces.

3 Plant flowers like pelargoniums, that can cope with hot dry places, and verbenas which will trail over the edge.

4 Squeeze in a pansy with a contrasting flower colour and a trailing lobelia plant. Lobelia grows in the smallest of spaces and will delicately tumble over the edge.

5 The boots need watering every day in the summer, and bloom even better if some plant food is mixed into the water once a week.

SAFETY NOTE
Children should always be supervised when using any sharp objects.

PLANT IN SPRING

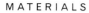

Watering Can Planter

An old watering can makes an attractive container, especially when it is painted and stencilled. When planted with an evergreen plant, such as the ivy used here, it will provide an eye-catching year-round display.

MATERIALS

Old watering can
Paintbrush
Eggshell paint, for the base coat
Stencil design
Masking tape
Stencil brush
Stencil paints, for the decoration
Fine paintbrush
Bark chippings
Slow-release plant food granules

PLANT

Ivy

1 Paint the watering can with the base colour. Apply two coats if necessary and leave each coat to dry thoroughly before painting the next.

2 Fasten the stencil design in place with masking tape. When stencilling, the brush should not hold much paint; dab it on newspaper to get rid of the excess. Use two or three colours to give your design a more three-dimensional effect.

GARDENER'S TIP

Other galvanized tin containers such as tin baths and buckets may also be painted and used.

PLANT AT ANY TIME OF THE YEAR

3 Use the fine paintbrush to paint the rim of the can. You could pick out additional detailing if you wish.

4 When all the paint is quite dry, fill the watering can with bark chippings.

5 Scoop out a hollow in the chippings and plant the ivy in its pot. Scatter some slow-release plant food granules on the surface. Arrange the tendrils so that they trail over the handle and spout of the watering can. Water, pouring any excess water out through the spout. Place the watering can in a shady spot or hang it from a hook in a cool corner.

Terrific Tyres

Old car tyres get a new and completely different lease of life with a lick of paint. They make perfect containers for all sorts of plants and are ideal for a first garden.

BEDDING PLANTS

MATERIALS

Coloured emulsion paints
Paintbrush
2 car tyres
Compost and garden soil
Newspaper

PLANTS

Selection of bedding plants such as cosmea pelargoniums, pansies (viola), and pot marigolds (calendula)

1 Use ordinary emulsion to paint the tyres – any colours look good, the brighter the better.

2 Put one tyre on top of another and fill with potting compost or equal quantities of garden soil and compost. To cut down on the amount of compost, stuff newspaper into the tyres.

3 Put the tallest plants in first – this is a cosmea. Surround it with smaller plants like pelargoniums, pansies and marigolds.

4 Plant some delicate trailing plants to grow over the edge. Start your tyre garden off by giving it a lot of water. Keep watering through the summer and do not let it get too dry.

GARDENER'S TIP

You can get old tyres for free at most garages. For something cheap and fast-growing, try growing pumpkin plants. A ring of lobelia will grow happily if planted between two tyres.

Seaside Garden

Even if you live miles from the sea you can create your own garden in a sunny corner with some seashells, succulents and driftwood.

MATERIALS

Seashells
Self-hardening clay
4 terracotta pots of various sizes
Loam-based compost with
  ¹⁄₃ added grit
Gravel
Driftwood

PLANTS

Gazania
3 mesembryanthemum
2 crassula
Upright lampranthus
2 trailing lampranthus

GAZANIA

LAMPRANTHUS

1 Fill the shells with clay, leaving some unfilled to cover the compost.

2 Press the shells onto the terracotta pots and leave the clay to harden overnight.

3 Plant the gazania in one of the larger pots.

4 Plant the three mesembryanthemums as a group in one pot.

5 Plant the crassulas together in a fairly small pot. These plants grow naturally in poor soils and do not mind overcrowding.

6 The upright and trailing lampranthus have similar colour foliage and flower but quite different shapes so they make an interesting contrast when planted together. Cover the compost in each pot with a layer of gravel and then add seashells and pieces of driftwood. Group together in a sunny position.

Good Enough to Eat!

You do not need a large garden to grow fruit and vegetables – it is possible to grow some in just a window box. Strawberries and bush or trailing tomatoes are small enough, so are radishes and lettuces. Nasturtium leaves and flowers are edible, with a hot, peppery taste. They look lovely in a salad.

MATERIALS

76 cm (30 in) plastic window box
Compost

PLANTS

2 tomato plants
2 strawberry plants
Radish seeds
Lettuce seeds
Nasturtium seeds

STRAWBERRY PLANTS

LETTUCE SEEDS

NASTURTIUM SEEDS

RADISH SEEDS

TOMATO PLANT

1 Fill the window box with compost to just below the rim. Plant the tomatoes in the back corners of the window box.

2 Plant the strawberries, about 30 cm (12 in) away from the tomatoes.

3 Sow radish and lettuce seeds 1 cm (½ in) apart. After the young radishes have been harvested, the lettuces can grow into their space.

4 Sow some nasturtium seeds in the corners so that they can grow up and trail over the edge. Water thoroughly.

GARDENER'S TIP

To get a plant out of a pot, turn it upside down with the stem between your fingers. With the other hand, firmly squeeze the bottom of the pot to release the rootball.

PLANT IN SPRING

A Watery World

No garden is complete without the sight and sound of water. Great for toe-dipping on a hot sunny day, this mini-pond is too small for fish but a welcome watering spot for thirsty birds. Any large container can be used to make a mini-pond, as long as it is watertight. A toy-tidy, like this one, is ideal.

MATERIALS

Large, wide container
Gravel
Lead from a wine bottle top
Flower pot

PLANTS

2 aquatic plants such as golden
*   sedge and monkey flower*
Strands of oxygenating weed
Small floating plants
*   such as water lettuce*
*   and floating ferns*

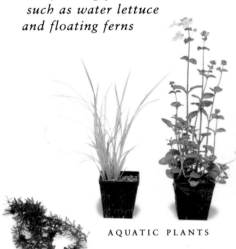

OXYGENATING
WEED

AQUATIC PLANTS

FLOATING
PLANTS

GARDENER'S TIP

Keep shallow containers in a semi-shady area to avoid excess evaporation. Plant up an adjoining mix of tulips and alliums for a spring and early summer display.

PLANT IN SPRING

1 Put a layer of gravel in the bottom of a large, wide container and fill with water almost to the top.

3 Bend a piece of lead around the base of pieces of oxygenating weed to weigh them down. Pot the bunch into a flower pot and put a layer of gravel on the surface.

2 Lower the aquatic plants (which should be in net pots when you buy them) gently into the water around the edge.

4 Lower the pot into the mini-pond, then add a few floating plants. Sink the pond into a hole in the garden so that it keeps cool.

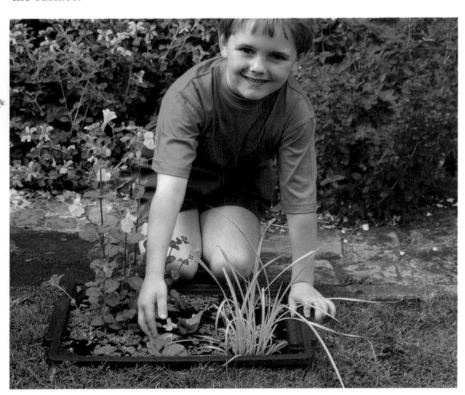

Indoor Containers

Plants do furnish a room, and the same considerations apply to the effective use of containers indoors as in the garden: find containers that suit their surroundings and the plants you have chosen for them; plant them imaginatively and group them for impact.

Foliage plants will form the backbone of most arrangements, rather as trees and shrubs do in the garden. Flowering plants won't be so long-lasting indoors, but are always the centre of attraction while they are in bloom.

Decorative pots intended to go outdoors can be used very successfully indoors too. Baskets make good plant holders if you line them with plastic. Your indoor plants will appreciate good light (although direct sunlight through glass is too powerful for most species) and a moist atmosphere: stand the pots in saucers of wet gravel and give them a daily misting to help keep them looking their best.

ABOVE: *Introduce flowering plants to your indoor collections to brighten up your home.*

Start a Collection

Once houseplants become more of a consuming hobby than a passing pleasure, you will begin to look for more ways to feed your passion. One option is to start a collection of a particular type of plants, whether a large and diverse group such as cacti, or a smaller, interesting group like saintpaulias (African violets).

SAINTPAULIAS

MATERIALS

Baskets or containers of various sizes
Florist's foam
Moss

PLANTS

Collection of plants, such as saintpaulias (African violets)

1 Start by grouping your plants to find an arrangement that pleases you.

2 The design will look more interesting if you can create a cascade effect using florist's foam to build up different levels.

3 Build up the back of the display on florist's foam first.

4 Fill in the space in front in steps. Try the plants for size so that you can use more foam beneath the pots if needed.

GARDENER'S TIP

To find the best range of plants, do not rely on the average garden centre. You must hunt out a specialist nursery where they will have a far more imaginative and superior collection: everything to satisfy the enthusiast.

PLANT IN EARLY SPRING

5 Arrange the plants to look as though they could be growing as a natural group and not in straight rows. Fill the spaces between the pots with moss.

Orchid Basket

MILTONIA

PLANTS

Miltonia or phalaenopsis orchid

Orchids are no longer the rare exotic plants that they used to be and most garden centres now stock some. A few inexpensive materials and a little time will create a stylish container to show these lovely flowers at their very best.

MATERIALS

Plastic-lined twig basket, 15 cm (6 in) diameter
Gravel
Sphagnum moss
3 x 40 cm (16 in) canes
Raffia

1 Pour a 2.5 cm (1 in) layer of gravel into the base of the basket and line with moss.

2 Slip the orchid (still in its pot) into the basket.

3 Push the canes into the moss at the edge of the basket so that they are held firmly in place.

4 Tie a length of raffia between each cane, finishing off with a neat knot.

GARDENER'S TIP

Orchids do not like to stand in water, but they do like a humid atmosphere. A layer of gravel underneath the pot acts as a reservoir for excess water which creates humidity. The orchid will also benefit from being sprayed with water.

PLANT AT ANY TIME OF THE YEAR

Colourful Kitchen Herbs

Make a bright cheerful statement by using painted tins as containers for your kitchen herbs, often now available in pots from most supermarkets.

PARSLEY

CORIANDER

BASIL

MATERIALS	PLANTS
Empty food tins	*Dill*
White spirit	*Chives*
Masking tape	*Parsley*
Paintbrush	*Coriander*
Gloss paint	*Basil*

GARDENER'S TIP

Large painted tins make colourful planters in the garden. Ask your local restaurant or school for some of the catering size tins that they normally throw away.

PLANT AT ANY TIME OF THE YEAR

1 Thoroughly wash and dry the tins. Use white spirit to remove any residual spots of glue. Wrap masking tape round the lips of the tins so that half of it protrudes above the rims.

2 Fold the protruding masking tape inside the rims of the tins.

3 Paint the tins and leave them to dry.

4 Depending on the colours you choose, some of them may need more than one coat. Leave to dry completely.

5 Place each plant, pot and all, in a separate tin. Stand in a light position and water if the compost dries out.

Period Fuchsias

Fuchsias were first cultivated in Europe in the 1780s. Many cultivars bred in the 1800s can still be found in cultivation today. Fuchsia 'Bland's New Striped' was first seen in cultivation in 1872, and 'Claire de Lune' in 1880. Growing plants from a particular period will add an exciting historic flavour to any collection.

MATERIALS

Victorian copper pot
Expanded clay granules
Victorian-style planter
Crocks
Compost

PLANTS

Fuchsia *'Claire de Lune'*
Fuchsia *'Bland's New Striped'*

1 Put a layer of expanded clay granules into the base of the Victorian copper pot. This will help to create a humid atmosphere around the plants.

2 Place the *Fuchsia* 'Claire de Lune' in the copper pot, arranging the branches and foliage to fall around the sides.

3 Cover the drainage hole in the bottom of the Victorian-style planter with terracotta crocks.

4 Fill the pot with compost.

5 Remove *F.* 'Bland's New Striped' from its pot. The network of fresh, healthy roots shows that the plant is strong and vigorous.

6 Plant in the compost. Cover the rootball and firm the compost with your hands.

GARDENER'S TIP

Orange flowers are often considered to be a modern advance in fuchsia cultivars, but 'Lye's Unique' has salmon-orange flowers, and originated in 1886. Other old varieties to look out for include 'Charming', a hardy bush which was developed in 1877.

PLANT IN EARLY SPRING OR EARLY SUMMER

Mixed Blessings

A bowl of mixed plants almost always looks better than the same number dotted around in individual pots. Garden centres and florists often sell mixed bowls, but you can probably make one more cheaply using a container that you already have – and you can ring the changes with different plants.

FOLIAGE AND
FLOWERING PLANTS

MATERIALS

Bowl with drainage hole
Crocks or bark chippings
Compost
Spare pot the same size as
  centrepiece plant pot

PLANTS

Collection of mixed foliage and
flowering plants

1 Cover the drainage hole with crocks or bark chippings. Part-fill the container with compost.

2 It is a good idea to have a showy centrepiece plant – insert an empty pot temporarily so that you are sure to leave enough space.

3 Place the other plants around the centrepiece, rearranging them as necessary while still in their pots. Do not start planting until you are happy with the results.

4 Remove the plants from their pots and plant. Finally, insert the centrepiece. If it is likely to be a long-term occupant, remove it from its pot. If you are likely to have to replace it after a few weeks – as is common with flowering plants once they finish blooming – keep it in its container.

GARDENER'S TIP

For a lively, varied mix use a combination of small bushy, vertical, and trailing plants. Tradescantias are a good choice for the last category, particularly since they come in a wide range of bright colours, including greens, creams and bronze.

PLANT AT ANY TIME OF YEAR

Water-loving Plants

The sweet flag is a marsh plant which loves the moist conditions in most bathrooms. Planted in gravel in a stylish glass pot or vase, it is easy to see when the water needs topping up.

MATERIALS

20 cm (8 in) glass vase or pot
Gravel

SWEET FLAG

PLANTS

1 large or 2 small sweet flags
(Acorus gramineus 'Variegatus')

1 Fill the bottom half of the container with gravel.

2 Take the plants out of their existing pots and place them on the gravel.

3 Fill the pot with gravel to the base of the leaves and half-fill the container with water. Place on a light window-sill and never allow the plants to dry out.

GARDENER'S TIP

The umbrella plant (Cyperus alternifolius) will also thrive in these conditions.

PLANT AT ANY TIME OF THE YEAR

Combined Effects

Displaying houseplants in groups creates a humid microclimate, which the plants prefer to the dry atmosphere of most homes. The humidity is increased by standing the pots in saucers of wet gravel kept moist by regular watering. Choose plants of contrasting shapes and sizes for the most striking effect.

MATERIALS

4 pots of various sizes with
*   saucers*
Crocks
Compost
Gravel

PLANTS

Lilies
Maidenhair fern
*   (adiantum)*
Cretan fern
Variegated creeping fig
*   (Ficus pumila)*

LILY

MAIDENHAIR FERN

CREEPING FIG

CRETAN FERN

1 Place the crocks in the bottom of the pots. Check the proportion of pot to plant.

3 Fill gaps around the rootballs with compost, pressing down firmly to avoid any air spaces.

5 Water the plants thoroughly. Fill the saucers with gravel. Stand the pots in their saucers and position the plants in good light, but away from direct sun. Keep the gravel in the saucers damp, and water the plants when the compost dries out.

2 Remove the lilies from their plastic container and position in the pot.

4 Remove the foliage plants from their containers and plant in the other pots, topping up with compost.

GARDENER'S TIP

Bear in mind the background of your display when choosing your plants. Large architectural leaves and strong plain colours won't get lost against a busy wallpaper, whereas lots of variegations and colour are better against a plain background.

PLANT AT ANY TIME OF THE YEAR

Plant Guide

Anemone blanda
Aquilegia alpina
*Arabis ferdinandi-
    coburgii* 'Variegata'
Asplenium crispum
Athyrium nipponicum
Berberis thunbergii
    'Atropurpurea Nana',
    B. darwinii
Bergenia
Box
*Ceratostigma
    plumbagoides*
*Chamaecyparis pisifera
    'Filifera Aurea,
    'Sungold'*
Choisya ternata
Convolvulus cneorum
Cotoneaster conspicuus
Crocus
Day lily
Dianthus
Dryopteris filix-mas
*Euonymous fortunei
    'Emerald and Gold'*
Euphorbia
Foxglove
Hebe
Helianthemum
Heuchera 'Palace
    Purple', 'Bressingham
    Bronze'
Holly
Hosta
Hydrangea
Inula
Iris reticulata
Ivy
Lamium
Lavender
Lily-of-the-valley
Narcissus
Nepeta mussinii
Ophiopogon planiscapus
    'Nigrescens'
Pachysandra terminalis
Polygonum affine
*Polystichum
    acrostichoides*
Potentilla
Primula auricula
Rosemary
Salix alpina
Sedum 'Ruby Glow'
Sedum ewersii
Sempervivum
Skimmia japonica
    'Rubella'
Thyme
*Trachelospermum
    jasminoides*
Veronica peduncularis
Vinca minor

TREES AND SHRUBS
FOR CONTAINERS

Acer palmatum
Apple (dwarf)
Bay
Berberis thunbergii
    'Atropurpurea Nana',
    B. darwinii
Box
Camellia
*Ceratostigma
    plumbagoides*
Chamaecyparis pisifera
Choisya ternata
*Citrus mitis**
Convolvulus cneorum
Cordyline*
Cotoneaster conspicuus
Datura*
Euonymous fortunei
Fuchsia
Hebe
Holly
Hydrangea
Lantana*
Lavender
Potentilla
Rhododendron
Rosemary
Rose
Skimmia

CLIMBERS FOR
CONTAINERS

Bougainvillea*
*Clematis alpina, C.
    macropetala*
*Cobaea scandens**
Gynura*
Ivy
Jasmine
Stephanotis*
Thunbergia alata
*Trachelospermum
    jasminoides*

TRAILING PLANTS FOR HANGING BASKETS

Ageratum*
Begonia semperflorens*
Bidens ferulifolia*
Brachycome iberidifolia
Campanula isophylla*
Chaenorhinum
  glareosum*
Convolvulus sabatius*
Erigeron mucronatus
Felicia*
Fuchsia (lax varieties)*
Gazania*
Glechoma hederacea
Helichrysum petiolare*

Lampranthus*
Lantana*
Lobelia*
Lotus berthelotti*
Lysimachia nummularia
Nasturtium
Osteospermum*
Pelargonium*
Petunia*
Sedum ewersii
Senecio maritima*
Sweet peas
Verbena*
Vinca minor

SPRING-FLOWERING PLANTS FOR CONTAINERS

Anagallis
Anemone blanda
Aquilegia
Arabis ferdinandi-
  coburgii 'Variegata'
Bluebells
Crocus
Day lily
Euphorbia
Forget-me-not
Iris reticulata

Lily-of-the-valley
Narcissus
Polyanthus
Primroses
Primula auricula
Snowdrops
Tulips
Vinca minor
Viola
Wallflower

AUTUMN AND WINTER COLOUR

Arabis ferdinandi-
  coburgii 'Variegata'
Berberis thunbergii
  'Atropurpurea Nana',
  B. darwinii
Bergenia
Ceratostigma
  plumbagoides
Chamaecyparis pisifera
  'Sungold'
Convolvulus cneorum
Euonymous fortunei
Euphorbia
Ferns
Heuchera 'Palace
  Purple', 'Bressingham
  Bronze'
Hakonechloa macra
  'Alboaurea'
Hebe
Holly
Iris unguicularis
Ivy
Pachysandra terminalis
Polygonum affine
Salvia greggii
Sedum 'Ruby Glow'
Vinca minor

*All plants marked with an asterisk need protection from frost

PLANTS FOR SHADE

Anemone blanda
Begonia semperflorens
Bergenia
Box
Campanula isophylla
Chamaecyparis pisifera
Digitalis
Euonymous
Euphorbia
Ferns
Glechoma hederacea
Heuchera
Holly
Hosta
Hydrangea
Impatiens*
Ivy
Lily-of-the-valley
Narcissus
Ophiopogon planiscapus
Pachysandra terminalis
Primrose
Primula auricula
Skimmia
Sorrel
Thunbergia alata
*Trachelospermum
   jasminoides*
Vinca minor
Viola

PLANTS FOR HOT CONDITIONS

Aloe*
Alyssum
Argyranthemum*
Arundinaria pygmaea
Crassula ovata
Diascia*
Erigeron mucronatus
Gazania*
*Hakonechloa macra
   'Aureola'*
Helianthemum
Inula
Lavender
Lotus berthelotti
Mesembryanthemum*
Osteospermum*

PLANTS WITH DECORATIVE FOLIAGE

Berberis thunbergii
Bergenia
Chamaecyparis pisifera
Choisya ternata
Convolvulus cneorum
Euonymous fortunei
Euphorbia
Fuchsia magellanica
Glechoma hederacea
Hebe
Hedera helix 'Hibernica'
Helichrysum petiolare
Heuchera
Holly
Hosta 'Blue Moon'
Lotus berthelotti
Lysimachia nummularia
Nasturtium 'Alaska'
Pachysandra terminalis
Pelargonium, ivy-leaved
Salvia officinalis
Senecio maritima
Thymus 'Silver Queen',
   'Archer's gold'
Vinca minor

FRAGRANT PLANTS

Alyssum
Bidens atrosanguinea
Cheiranthus
Choisya ternata
Citrus mitis
Dianthus
Heliotrope
Jasmine
Lavender
Lilies
Lily-of-the-valley
Nicotiana
Pelargonium, scented-
   leaved varieties*
Rosemary
Sweet pea
Thyme
*Trachelospermum
   jasminoides*
Viola odorata

Index

Below *Begonia*

Above *Hyacinthus*

ACKNOWLEDGEMENTS
All projects were created by
Stephanie Donaldson and
photographed by Marie O'Hara
unless stated below.

Contributors
Clare Bradley: 76, 77, 80, 81.
Kathy Brown: 4, 5, 6b, 95, 96.
Blaise Cooke: 12, 13, 86, 87.
Tessa Evelegh: 8, 9.
Peter McHoy: 83, 88.

Photographers
John Freeman: 12, 13, 14, 17r,
18r, 19mr, 35, 36, 37, 45, 53, 68,
70, 71, 73, 74, 75, 76, 77, 80, 81,
84, 85, 86, 87, 89, 90, 91.
Michelle Garrett: 4, 5, 6b, 95, 96.
Don Last: 83, 88.
Debbie Patterson: 8, 9, 18l.